Small and TALL Dinosaurs

By

Emily Kington

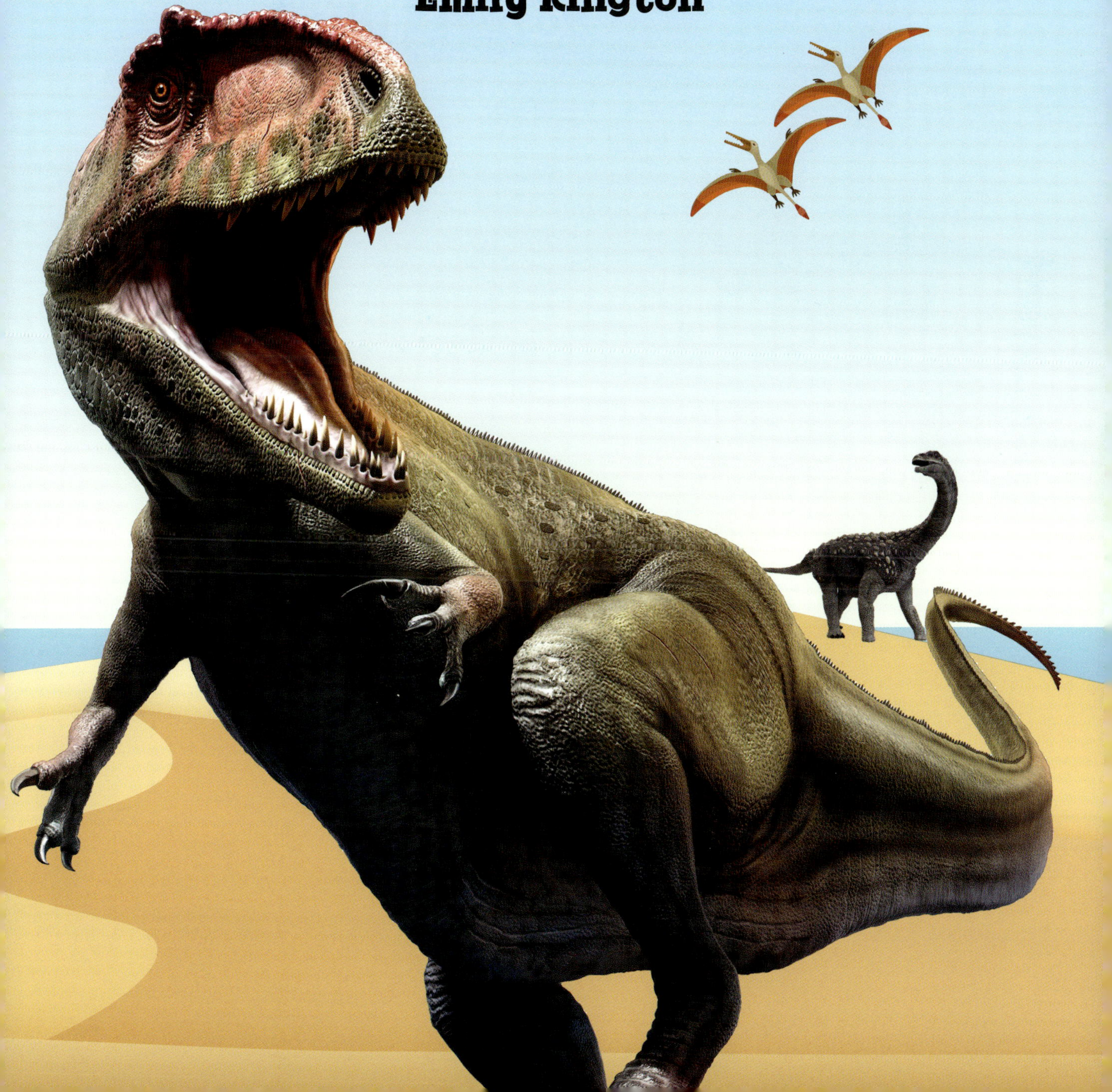

CONTENTS

First published in Great Britain in 2019 by Hungry Tomato Ltd
PO Box 181, Edenbridge, Kent, TN8 9DP

ISBN 978-1-912108-37-4

Discover more at
www.hungrytomato.com

SMALL AND TALL DINOSAURS

Dinosaurs lived around the world millions of years ago. They needed to live where there was enough food.

Dinosaur fossils of all shapes and sizes have been found. We can tell that some dinosaurs were . . .

. . . small **and some were very TALL.**

ARGENTINOSAURUS

AHR-gen-TEEN-uh-SAWR-us

Argentinosaurus **may be the largest plant-eating dinosaur discovered.**

Because of their size, they probably moved slowly, about 5 mph, which is as fast as a turtle!

Only pieces of *Argentinosaurus* fossils have been recovered, so its size has been estimated.

They lived 100 million years ago in Argentina.

Argentinosaurus eggs were about a foot (30.5 cm) in diameter.

GIGANOTOSAURUS

jye-gah-NOH-te-SAWR-us

Giganotosaurus **is one of the largest known meat-eating dinosaurs in South America.**

They may have been a monster-size and fierce to look at, but they had a brain the size of a banana!

Giganotosaurus had three-fingered clawed hands and longer arms than T-rex.

They were slightly bigger than a T-rex.

They lived 95 million years ago in South America.

SCALE

TITANOSAURUS

ty-TAN-uh-SAWR-us

***Titanosaurus* were some of the biggest animals to walk on our planet.**

They had armored skin. This protected them against attacks from **predators.**

They lived 70 million years ago in North America, India, and Europe.

They had very long necks and tails but very small heads.

Titanosaurus were quadrupeds, which means they walked on four legs.

MICRORAPTOR

MY-kro-rap-tor

Microraptor **was a small, bird-like dinosaur with four wings.**

There were probably lots of small *Microraptors* around. Over 300 fossils have been found.

It would have been difficult for *Microraptor* to walk on land because their wings were attached to their feet.

They lived 130 million years ago in China.

They had long feathers on their arms, tail, and legs.

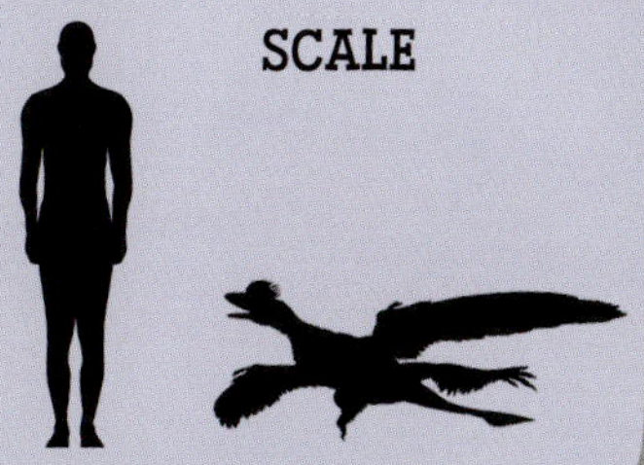

SAUROPOSEIDON

SAWR-oh-po-SY-den

Sauroposeidon **is not the largest dinosaur, but it is the tallest dinosaur ever known.**

Sauroposeidon means earthquake god reptile.

This tall dinosaur could probably raise its head 59 ft (18 m) from the ground. That's about the length of a bowling lane.

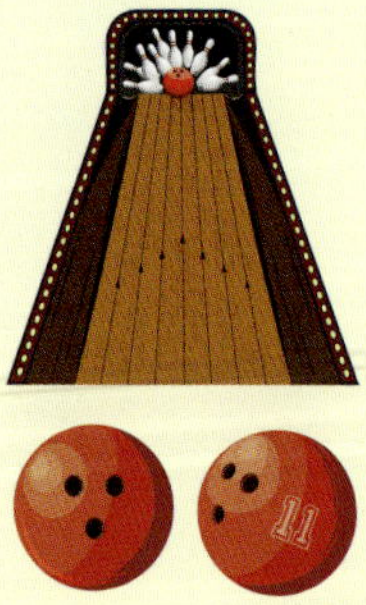

You can definitely call this a long-neck dinosaur. Its neck grew to 39 feet (12 m) long!

They lived 112 million years ago in USA.

The bones inside the neck were very light and thin like the bones of a chicken.

Scientist believe the ground shook as this dinosaur walked.

QUETZALCOATLUS

KWET-zal-koh-AT-lus

***Quetzalcoatlus* was a flying lizard and the largest known creatures ever to fly.**

Scientists believe they may have fed like storks on the ground, folding their huge wings and using them for balance.

They were about the size of a small aircraft.

They lived 68 million years ago in North America.

They had hollow bones like a modern-day bird and a 40-foot (12 m) wingspan.

Quetzalcoatlus was named after a mythical serpent god of Mexico.

SCALE

SALTASAURUS

salt-uh-SAWR-us

***Saltasaurus* was the smallest titanosaur, but they would still be giants if they were around today.**

Saltasaurus was half the length of *Argentinosaurus* but still weighed as much as 10 tons!

They had crocodile-like armor to protect them when under attack.

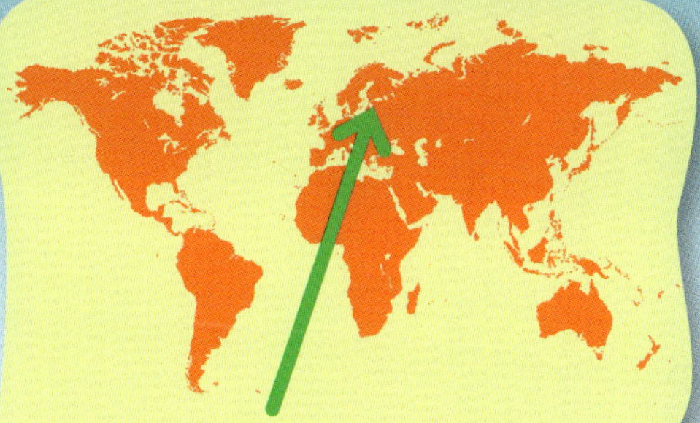

They lived 70 million years ago in Argentina.

They probably would have needed to eat around 400 pounds (181 kg) of vegetation a day.

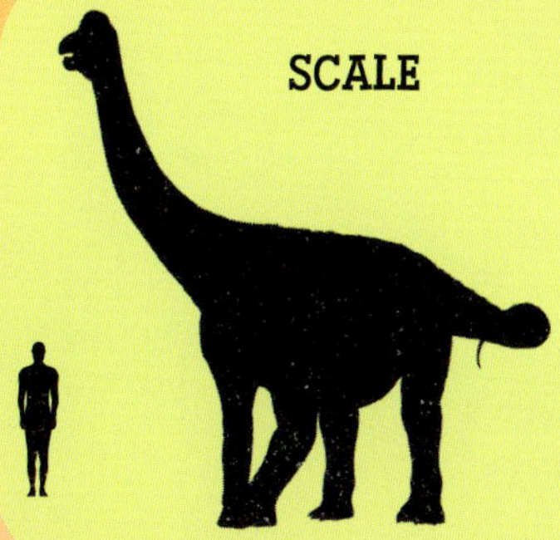

DILONG

dih-LONG

***Dilong* is the smallest tyrannosaur to ever be discovered.**

They lived 123 million years ago in China.

Young *Dilong* was covered with simple feathers, which may have kept them warm.

They had more developed arms than a giant T-rex.

Dilong means emperor dragon
They weighed about 12 pounds (5 kg) about the same as 3 bags of sugar.
SCALE

EUROPASAURUS

yoo-roh-pah-SAWR-us

Europasaurus **may have been small because there was less food available where they lived.**

They were only 20 feet (6 m) long.

They had a ridge on the top of their nose.

They lived 154 million years ago in Germany.

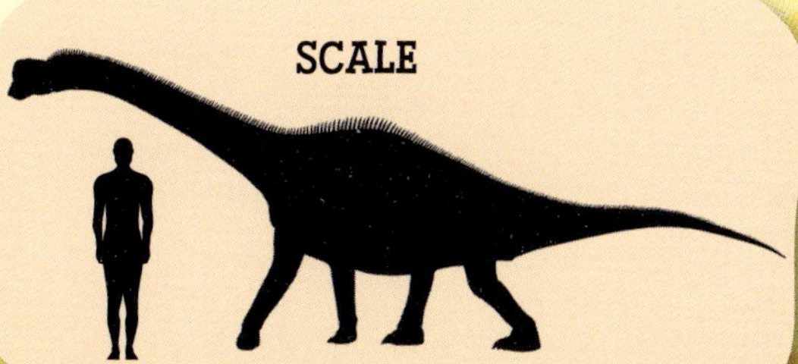

They were small for sauropods, about the size of a large ox.

GLOSSARY

armored: protected by or equipped with a defensive covering

estimate: an opinion or judgement, an approximation

plunderer: someone who robs or steals something, especially by force

predators: animals that live mostly by killing and eating other animals

vegetation: plant life or cover

Picture credits
Shutterstock. Warpaint 1, 6-7, 12-13, 14-15, 18-19. Herschel Hoffmeyer: 1, 4-5, 8-9, 16-17. Daniel Eskridge 2-3. Zhogolev_PV 6. Isaeva Anna 8. Catmando 10-11, 2021. R oi and Roi 14. Curiosity 18. ImissisHope 20. Michael Rosskothen Michael Rosskothen Michael Rosskothen Michael Rosskothen Michael Rosskothen Michael Rosskothen 22-23. Weberjake 22. Lemberg Vector studio. AnnstasAg. Ideyweb. HappyPictures. ONYXprj. Tatyana Gavrilova. Nadia Snopek. Evgenia L. Kheat. Droidworker. KANCHIT. Tinkivink.

Every effort has been made to trace the copyright holders, and we apologize in advance for any unintentional omissions. We would be pleased to insert the appropriate acknowledgements in any subsequent edition of this publication.